About the Author

Irene Daria, Ph.D. is a developmental psychologist who specializes in teaching children how to read.

In addition to teaching the children of many celebrities to read, she has taught hundreds of other children—both as a paid specialist and as a volunteer—and has trained teachers in the science of reading.

A passionate literacy advocate, Dr. Daria is the founder and director of Steps Tutoring in New York City. Her *Steps to Reading* workbook series will enable you to teach a child how to read using the same research-based, fun, and effective methods Dr. Daria uses in her renown private lessons.

For more information, visit:
www.StepsTutoring.com or www.StepstoReading.com.

Bulk discounts are available. Please email: info@StepsPublishing.com

For more information about Steps to Reading see:
www.StepstoReading.com

Copyright @2024 by STEPS Publishing, Inc. All rights reserved. No part of this book may be reproduced or utilized in any form or by any electronic or mechanical means, including photocopying, without permission in writing from the publisher.

Printed in the U.S.A.
ISBN 978-0-9864329-8-9

Book 3

STEPS to...
Reading

by Irene Daria, Ph.D.

Illustrations by Tingting Wei, Eryka Sajek, and Eric Wiener

Table of Contents

The sound of -ch .... Pg. 2

Sight word: have .... Pg. 16

The sound of –sh .... Pg. 34

Sight word: out .... Pg. 46

The sound of –th .... Pg. 54

Sight word: all .... Pg. 66

The sound of –wh .... Pg. 78

Sight word: what .... Pg. 82

What this book teaches

This is Book 3 in the Steps to Reading series. This book teaches digraphs. These are the sounds "ch," "sh," "th" and "wh."

      This book builds on the skills taught in Steps to Reading Book 1 and Book 2. Book 1 teaches children short vowels in three-letter words like "cat" and "hop." Book 2 teaches blends. These are longer words like "clap" and "hand" in which two consonants at the beginning and/or end of words are sounded out. If your student has not yet mastered short vowels or blends, complete Steps to Reading Book 1 and/or Book 2 before doing this book.

Supplemental materials

The books listed below are great practice for the skills your student will be learning as he or she progresses through the lessons in this book.

- "The Alphabet Series, Volume 1," compiled by Frances Bloom. This is a set of 18 little books published by Educators Publishing Service. If you have used Steps to Reading Books 1 and 2 with your student, then you probably already have this set. We will be using three of them ("Chip Had a Hut," "Tish the Fish," and "A Wish for Yak") with this workbook.

- "One Fish, Two Fish, Red Fish, Blue Fish," by Dr. Seuss.

- "Now I'm Reading! Level One: Animal Antics." This is an e-book set of early readers by Nora Gaydos from Random House. There are several "Level One" sets. Make sure you buy the one called "Animal Antics."

Step 1   The sound of 'ch'

'ch' says
'ch' as in chick

Instructions

Say to the child: "**When the letters c and h stand side by side, you do not sound them out. Instead, they combine to make a special sound. They say, 'ch' as in the words chick and chin.**"

ch words

Say: **"Circle the letters at the beginning of the word the picture shows."**
Tell the child the pictures show: chip, chick, chin, chop, check, and chimp.

Write a word

Say: "**Write 'ch' on the lines and read the words out loud.**"

__in	__ip
__at	__ill
in__	pin__
__eck	ben__

Which word is it?

Say: "**Read each word out loud. Circle the word that goes with the picture.**"

chin   chop

chick   chuck

chimp   chomp

chop   chip

chill   check

bench   punch

Write the word and circle the picture

Say: "Read the word out loud. Then write the word, and circle the picture that shows the word."

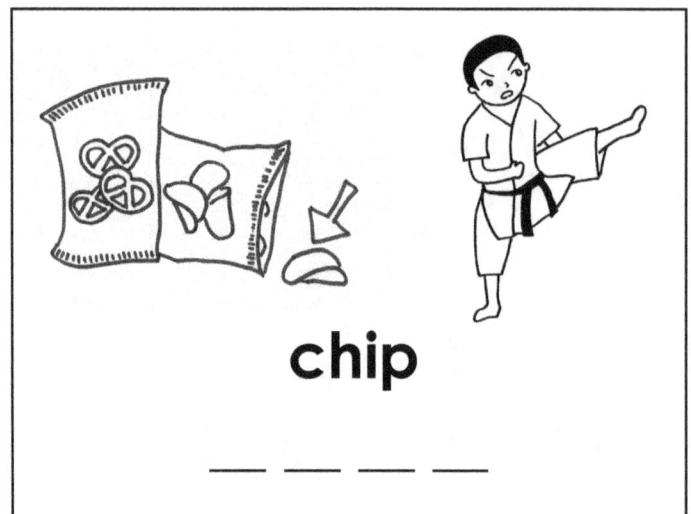

chip

_ _ _ _

chop

_ _ _ _

chimp

_ _ _ _ _

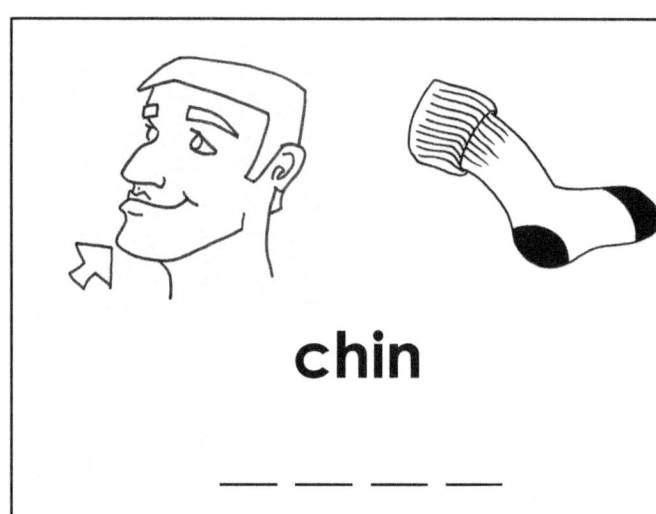

chin

_ _ _ _

chick

_ _ _ _ _

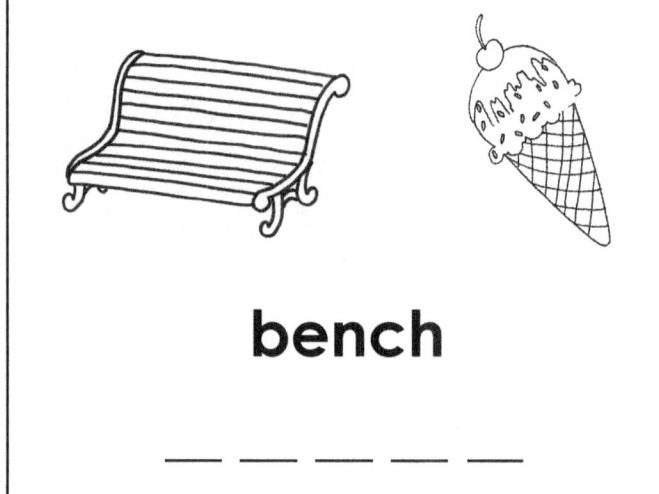

bench

_ _ _ _ _

Draw a line from the word to the picture

Say: "**Read each word out loud. Then draw a line from the correct word to the picture.**"

chip
chop
chap

limp
chimp
chomp
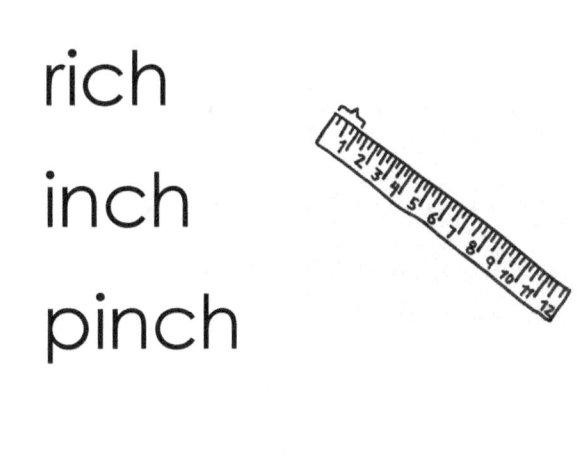

pin
chin
slim

rich
inch
pinch

peck
deck
check

bench
bunch
pinch

Vocabulary

chat
To talk.

Example: **I had a chat with my friend.**

bunch
A group of the same thing.

Example: **I ate a bunch of grapes.**

chill
To make colder.

Example: **I need to chill the lemonade.**

chuck
To throw.

Example: **Chuck the ball over here.**

chimp
An ape.

Example: **The chimp in the zoo is so cute!**

chomp
To chew loudly.

Example: **He chomped as he ate the sandwich.**

Circle the letters

Say: "**Circle the correct letters. Then write the word.**"
Tell the child the pictures show: inch, chimp, chip, bench, chin, check.

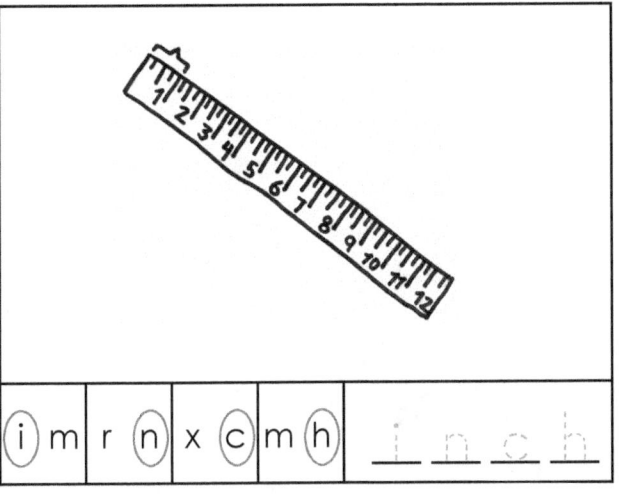

(i) m r (n) x (c) m (h)   _i_ _n_ _c_ _h_

(ch) i w n m g p   _ _ _ _ _ _

k c h i x m p   _ _ _ _ _

b s i e n i (ch)   _ _ _ _ _ _

k c r h x i m n   _ _ _ _ _

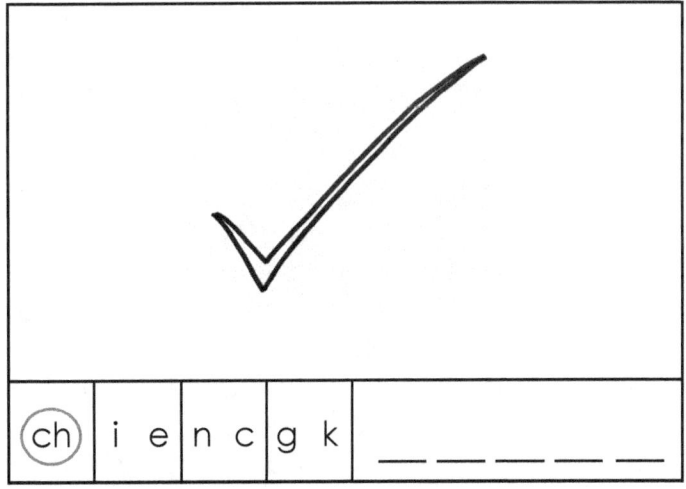

(ch) i e n c g k   _ _ _ _ _ _

9

Play Bingo with "ch" words

Instructions

Materials:
- Flashcards. Cut out the cards on the opposite page.
- 2 gameboards follow the flashcards. In Bingo, every player gets his or her own gameboard. You and the child should each select a gameboard to use.
- Pennies to use as game pieces.

1. Place the flashcards in one stack, with the words facing up.
2. Have the child read the word on the top card in the stack.
3. Each of you should look for that word on your Bingo boards and place a penny on top of the word on your boards when you find it.
4. Place the card the child read face down on the table.
5. Repeat steps 2-4. The child should be the one doing all of the reading of the words on the flashcards. Continue until one of you has three pennies in a row, either horizontally, vertically, or diagonally. The first player to get three in a row should call out, "Bingo!" That player wins the game.

Bingo Flashcards

Cut out the cards along the dotted lines.

chin	chip	chat
chill	check	inch
chimp	bench	pinch

This page is intentionally left blank.

This page is intentionally left blank.

BINGO

chin	chip	chat
chill	check	inch
chimp	bench	pinch

BINGO

check	chimp	inch
chat	chin	bench
chip	pinch	chill

Step 2

What you need to know about...
Sight Words

Sight Words are words the child needs to memorize, as opposed to sound out. Sight words either do not follow phonics rules (and, therefore, cannot be sounded out) or they are very common words that follow phonics rules the child has not yet learned.

The sight words in this book are presented in the order they will appear in the stories children will be reading as they make their way through this book. I call them Power Words because knowing how to read these sight words will increase the child's reading power. Since these words are so common in stories, memorizing them will enable your child to read many books much more quickly.

If your student completed the first two books in the Steps to Reading series, then he or she knows the 24 most common sight words. (They are listed on the following pages.) If your student did not complete Book 1 or 2, make sure your student knows those words before proceeding.

First set of Power Words

the	has	off
is	to	his
on	was	dog
as	of	for

Second set of Power Words

see	down	little
says	put	with
go	pull	look
no	full	said

Power Word

Instructions

1. Say: "**Some words don't follow any of the sounding out rules. They are words that just need to be memorized. We will call them Power Words because they are words that appear very often in the stories you will be reading. Knowing these words will really boost your reading power.**"
2. Point to the word "have," *above*. Say, "**This word is 'have.'**"
3. On the following page, your student will trace and write the word "have."
4. Any time you come to a Power Word lesson in this book, read the word to the child and have him or her trace and write the word on the lines that follow.

Write the Word

have

have

have

have

have

have

Does the sentence make sense?

Say: "**Read each sentence out loud. Color in the smiley face if the sentence makes sense and the frown if it does not.**"

I have a rich chimp that is sick, said the fox.	☺	☹

I have to say cluck, said the chick.	☺	☹

I have to chomp on the chip, said the man.	☺	☹

I have to pinch his chin, said the chimp.	☺	☹

I have to punch the mat, said the chick.	☺	☹

I have to peck the stamp, said the chick.	☺	☹

I have a bunch of chicks that did swim, said the man.	☺	☹

I have to chop the block, said the duck.	☺	☹

Play the "ch" board game

Instructions

Materials you will need:
- A single die.
- Coins to use as markers.
- Gameboard, *opposite page*.

1. Each player places a coin on "start."
2. Take turns rolling the die.
3. Move forward the same amount of spaces as the number on the die.
4. As you move forward on the board, read the words that you pass and land on.
5. For example, if a five comes up on the die, move five spaces on the game board and read five words.
6. The first person to reach the end wins.

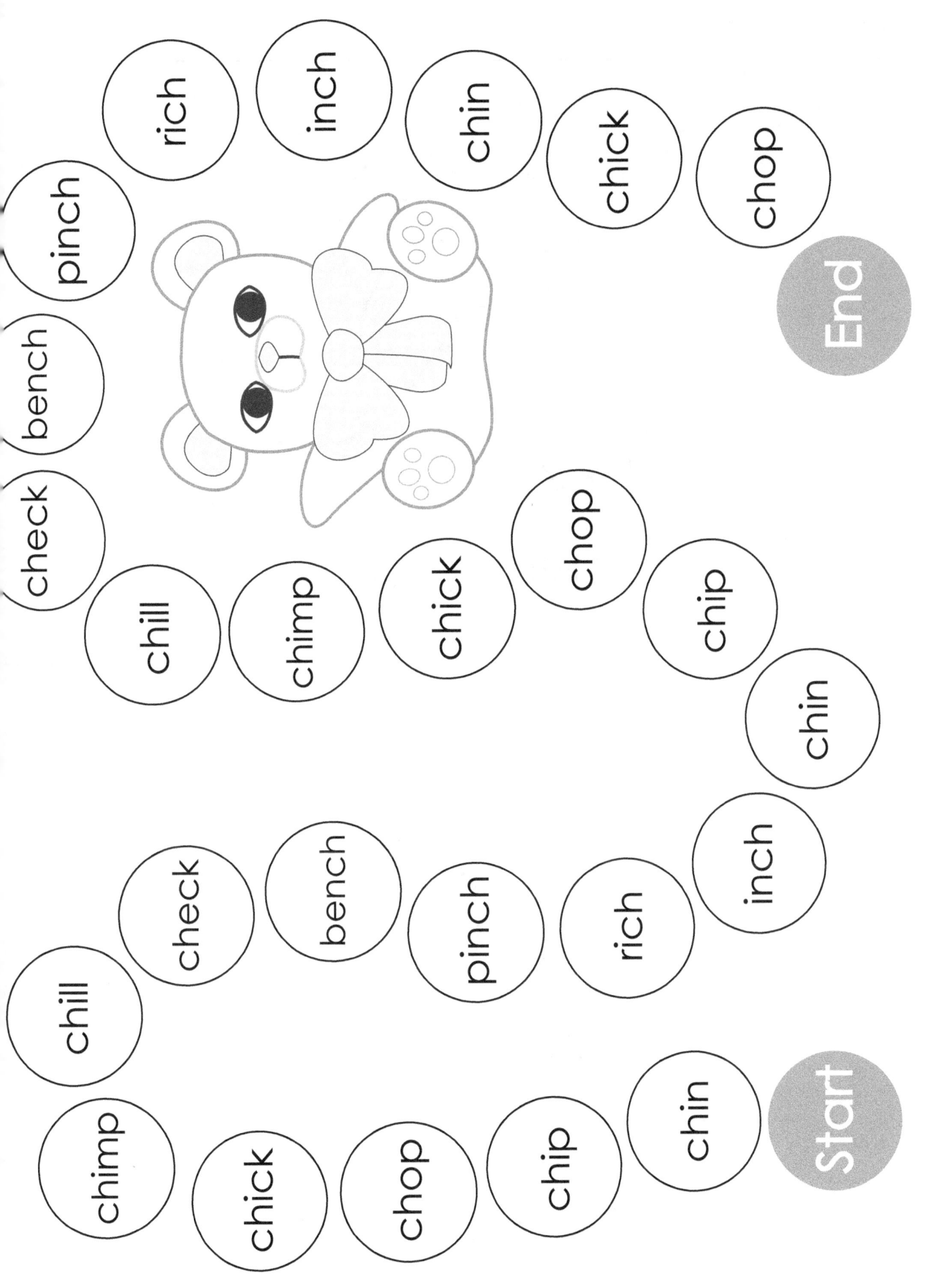

Read a story!

This is Chick.

Chick was sad.

Chick and Hal

Then Chick got a pal.

This is Hal.

Read a story!

All is well.

They have fun.

26

Chick and Hal

They run.

They kick the ball.

Read a story!

They jump and skip.

Hal's pants rip.

Chick and Hal

They went back.

And got a sack.

Read a story!

He put it on.

And had more fun!

ch puzzle

Word Box

bunch
chick
chimp
pinch
chin
check
chill
bench
chop
chip

Across

1. A seat for more than two people.
4. An ape.
5. A written mark that means something is correct.
6. The bottom of your face.
7. To cut into smaller pieces.

Down

1. Three of more of something.
2. A baby chicken.
3. To squeeze between two fingers.
5. To make colder.
6. A salty snack food.

ch puzzle answers

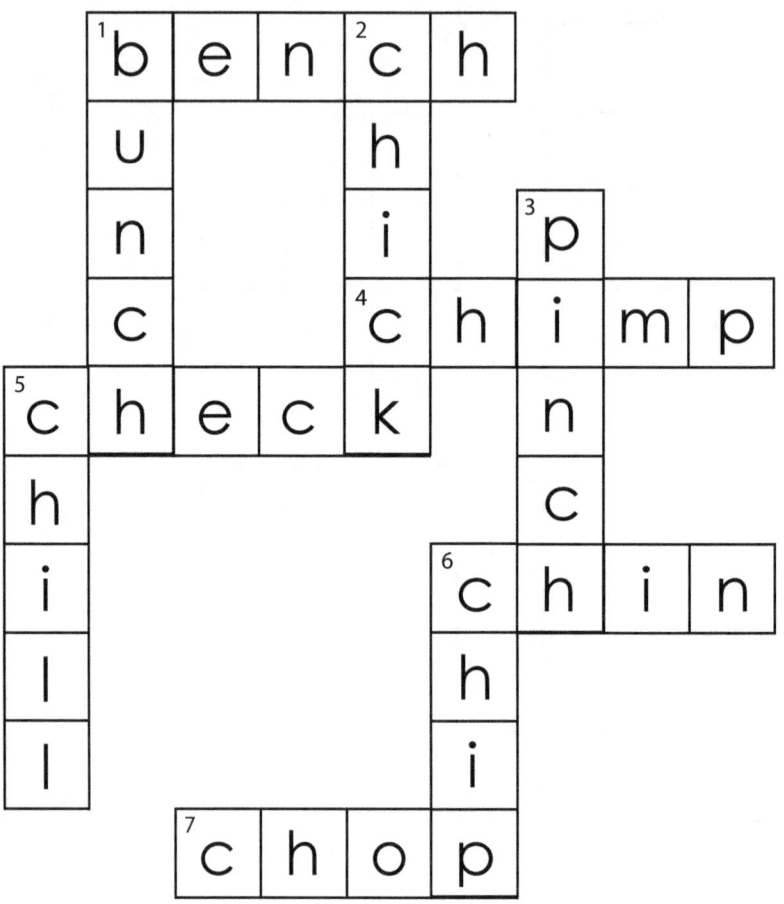

Read a book!

Instructions

Read a book

The child should read:

- "Chip Had a Hut," by Mary Geiger.
  This is book 7 in The Alphabet Series.
  See "Supplemental Materials," p. 1.

Step 3 — The sound of 'sh'

'sh' says
'sh' as in ship

Instructions

Say to the child: "**The letters 'sh' say 'sh' as in the words ship, shop, and shell.**"

sh words

Say: "**For the top two pictures, circle the letters you hear at the beginning of each word. The pictures show the words ship and shell.** For the rest of the words, circle the letters you hear at the end of the words. The pictures show cash, fish, dish, and trash."

35

Write a word

Say: "**Write 'sh' on the blank lines and read the words out loud.**"

__ip	__op
__ed	di__
fi__	wi__
__ack	__ell

Which word is it?

Say: **"Read each word out loud. Circle the word that goes with the picture."**

ship   slip

mash   cash

fish   wish

tell   shell

trash   track

wish   dish

Write the word and circle the picture

Say: "Read the word out loud. Then write the word, and circle the picture that shows the word."

fish

_ _ _ _

dish

_ _ _ _

cash

_ _ _ _

ship

_ _ _ _

trash

_ _ _ _ _

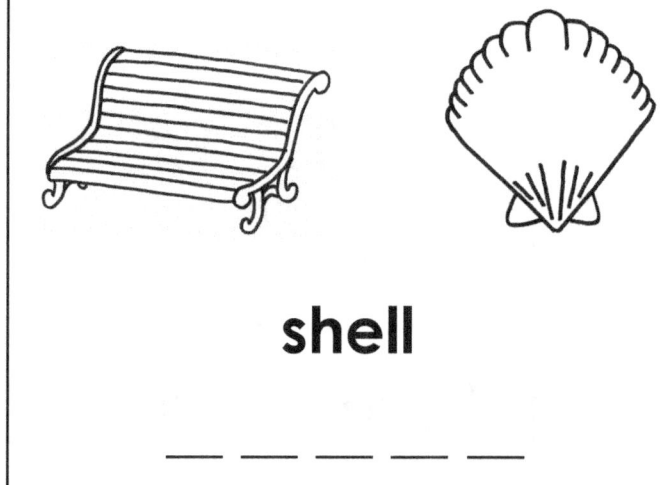

shell

_ _ _ _ _

Draw a line from the word to the picture

Say: "**Read each word out loud.** Then draw a line from the correct word to the picture."

wish
fish
dish

shop
stop
ship

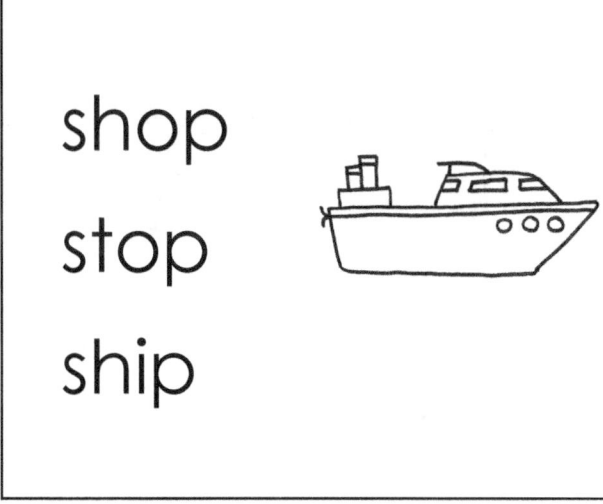

rash
cash
mash

dish
hush
wish

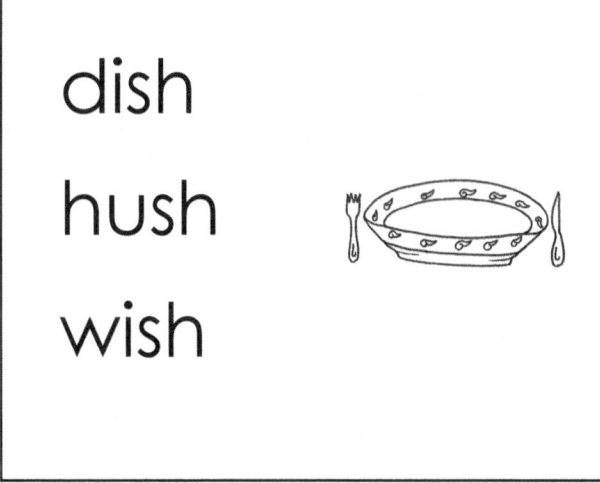

shed
trash
shin

shock
shell
smell

Circle the letters

Say: "**Circle the correct letters. Then write the word.**"
Tell the child the pictures show: dish, fish, ship, cash, shell, trash.

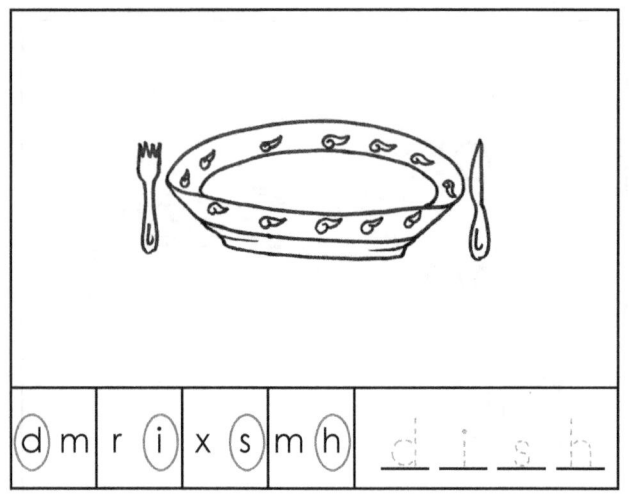

(d) m r (i) x (s) m (h)   d i s h

f m e i n s h x   _ _ _ _

k s h i x i m p   _ _ _ _

k c h a x s m h   _ _ _ _

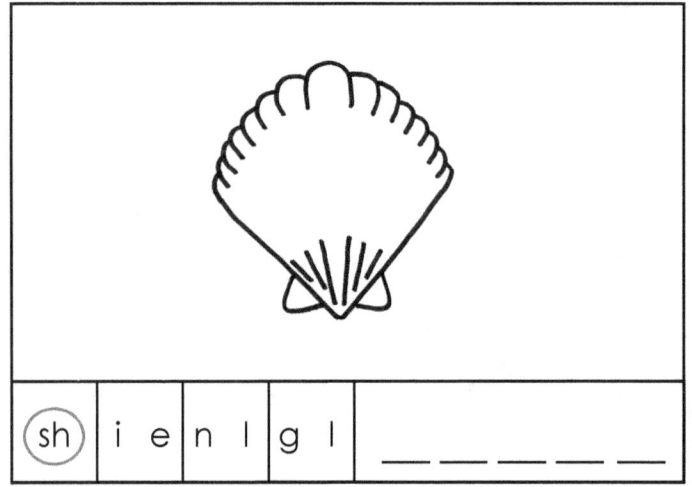

(sh) i e n l g l   _ _ _ _ _

t k r e a c (sh)   _ _ _ _ _

Play Bingo!

This Bingo game reinforces the sounds of "sh" and "ch." Cut out the flashcards on this page and play using the two Bingo boards on the following pages. (The big X in the center of each of the gameboards that follow is a "free" space. Each of you can use that space on your boards to get five in a row.) Have fun!

shop	chop	ship	chip

shin	chin	shed	chat	shell
chop	shock	chant	cash	chill
bash	inch	mash	rich	wish
bench	dish	hush	pinch	trash

This page is intentionally left blank.

This page is intentionally left blank.

BINGO

shop	chop	ship	chip	chop
shin	chin	shed	chat	shell
shock	chant	✗	cash	chill
bash	inch	mash	rich	wish
bench	dish	hush	pinch	trash

BINGO

shin	chin	shell	cash	chip
chop	shop	chill	shed	bash
inch	chat	✕	chop	mash
dish	ship	chant	shock	pinch
hush	rich	bench	wish	trash

Step 4　　　　　　　　　　　　　Power Word

out

out

out

out

Does the sentence make sense?

Say: "**Read each sentence out loud. Color in the smiley face if the sentence makes sense and the frown if it does not.**"

Put out the trash in the bag. ☺ ☹

The fish did wish to go out. ☺ ☹

Pull out the dish. ☺ ☹

The duck did wish to pull out the cash. ☺ ☹

The chick did pull out the shell. ☺ ☹

Put out the fish in the shop. ☺ ☹

Pull out the bench. ☺ ☹

Pull out the cash in the bank. ☺ ☹

Play the "sh" and "ch" board game!

First one to reach the end wins!

| Instructions |

Materials you will need: • A single die.
• Coins to use as markers.
• Gameboard, *opposite page*.

1. Each player places a coin on "start."
2. Take turns rolling the die.
3. Move forward the same amount of spaces as the number on the die.
4. As you move forward on the board, read the words that you pass and land on.
5. For example, if a five comes up on the die, move five spaces on the game board and read five words.
6. The first person to reach the end wins.

Vocabulary

shed

A small building used to store things.

Example: **He kept his tools in the shed.**

shin

The front of your leg from knee to ankle.

Example: **His shin was bruised.**

stash

To store.

Example: **Stash your shoes in the closet.**

hush

Hush.

Example: **A hush fell over the crowd.**

smash

To bang hard.

Example: **He smashed his thumb with the hammer.**

shack

A small house.

Example: **He lived in a shack in the woods.**

sh puzzle

Across

3. Red bumps on skin.
4. The outside of an egg.
5. Money.
6. A small building usually used for storage.
7. To want something.
8. To buy things in a store.

Down

1. An animal that lives under water.
2. Garbage.
6. A big boat.
9. Another word for plate.

Word Box

trash
shell
fish
rash
cash
shed
wish
ship
dish
shop

sh puzzle answers

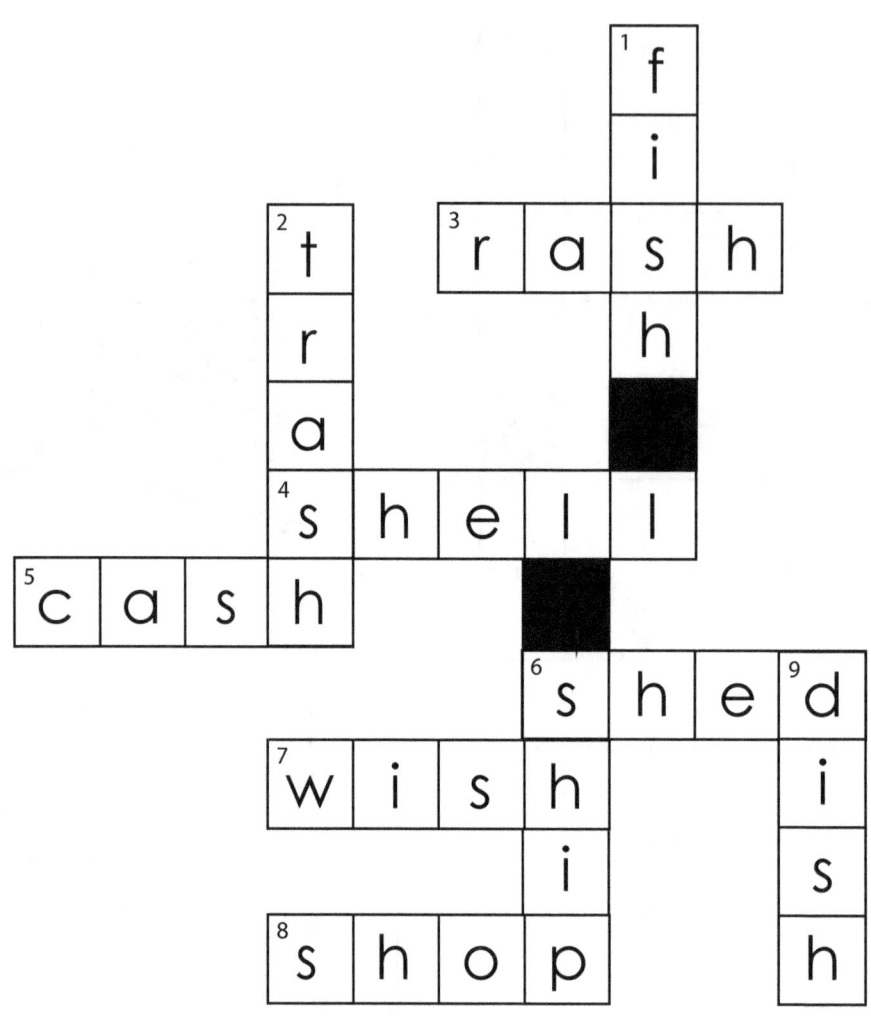

Read a book!

Instructions

Read a book

The child can now read:

- "Fish Gift." This is book 8 in the "Animal Antics" set by Nora Gaydos.

- "Tish the Fish." This is book 14 in the Alphabet Series.

Step 5   The sound of 'th'

'th' says
'th' as in thorn

Instructions

Say to the child: "**The letters 'th' say 'th' as in the words the, that, and thorn.**"

th words

Say: "For the top four pictures, circle the letters you hear at the end of each word. The pictures show: teeth, bath, math, and path. For the last two pictures, circle the letters you hear at the beginning of thick and think."

ch   th

th   sh

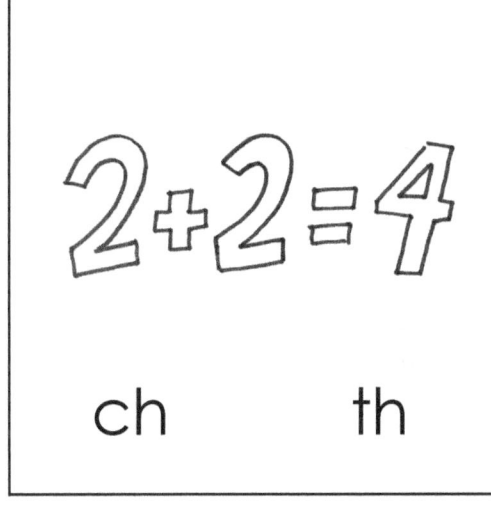

ch   th

th   sh

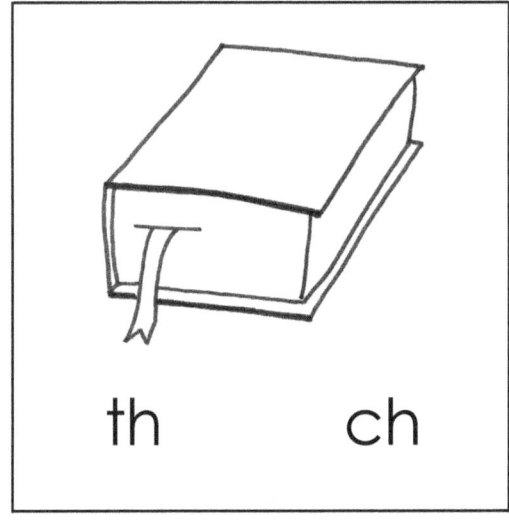

th   ch

th   sh

55

Write a word

Say: **"Write 'th' on the blank lines and read the words out loud."**

__e	__at
__is	__em
__en	ba__
pa__	ma__

Which word is it?

Say: **"Read each word out loud. Circle the word that goes with the picture."**

bath   math

teeth   tuck

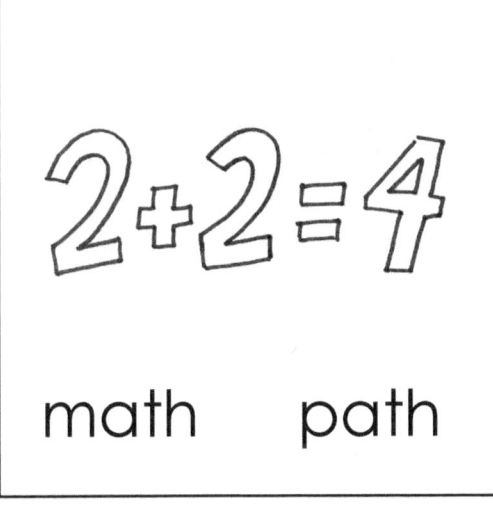

math   path

bath   path

thick   slick

think   ring

Write the word and circle the picture

Say: "Read the word out loud. Then write the word, and circle the picture that shows the word.

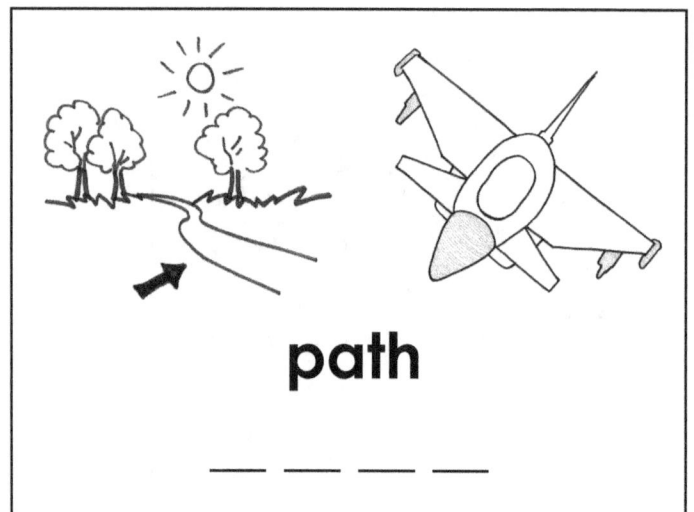

path

___ ___ ___ ___

bath

___ ___ ___ ___

math

___ ___ ___ ___

teeth

___ ___ ___ ___ ___

thick

___ ___ ___ ___ ___

think

___ ___ ___ ___ ___

Draw a line from the word to the picture

Say: "**Read each word out loud. Then draw a line from the correct word to the picture.**"

bath math path	meet teeth sweet 
this them path 	bath that math 
sick thick slick 	drink think thank 

Play "th," "ch," and "sh" Bingo

Instructions

Materials:
- Flashcards. Cut out the cards on the opposite page.
- 2 gameboards follow the flashcards. In Bingo, every player gets his or her own gameboard. You and the child should each select a gameboard to use.
- Pennies to use as game pieces.

1. Place the flashcards in one stack, with the words facing up.
2. Have the child read the word on the top card in the stack.
3. Each of you should look for that word on your Bingo boards and place a penny on top of the word on your boards when you find it.
4. Place the card the child read face down on the table.
5. Repeat steps 2-4. The child should be the one doing all of the reading of the words on the flashcards. Continue until one of you has five pennies in a row, either horizontally, vertically, or diagonally. The first player to get five in a row should call out, "Bingo!" That player wins the game.

Play Bingo!

the	bath	that	chip

this	chick	them	ship	then
shop	thin	chat	thick	chill
think	shell	thank	fish	thing
dish	path	check	math	wish

This page is intentionally left blank.

This page is intentionally left blank.

BINGO

the	bath	that	chip	this
chick	them	ship	then	shop
thin	chat	✕	thick	chill
think	shell	thank	fish	thing
dish	path	check	math	wish

BINGO

this	shell	then	dish	chip
chat	the	fish	ship	thin
them	path	✕	bath	thank
that	chick	think	shop	chill
thing	math	thick	check	wish

Step 6 — Power Word

all

all

all

all

all

Make words that end with -all

Say: "**Write the word 'all' on the blank lines. Then read each word out loud.**"

b _ _ _	c _ _ _
f _ _ _	h _ _ _
t _ _ _	w _ _ _
m _ _ _	sm _ _ _

Read a story!

This is a small ball.

That is a big ball.

This and That

This is a small wall.

That is a big wall.

Read a story!

This is a small fish.

That is a big fish.

This and That

This is a small duck.

That is a big duck.

Read a story!

This is a small cat.

That is a big cat.

th puzzle

Word Box

teeth
thanks
thick
think
math
path
thin
bath

Across

2. You use your brain to ____.
3. A word you say when you are grateful.
6. A small road.
7. What you take in a big tub of water.

Down

1. What you chew with.
2. The opposite of thin.
4. A subject you study in school that involves numbers.
5. Another word for someone who is skinny.

th puzzle answers

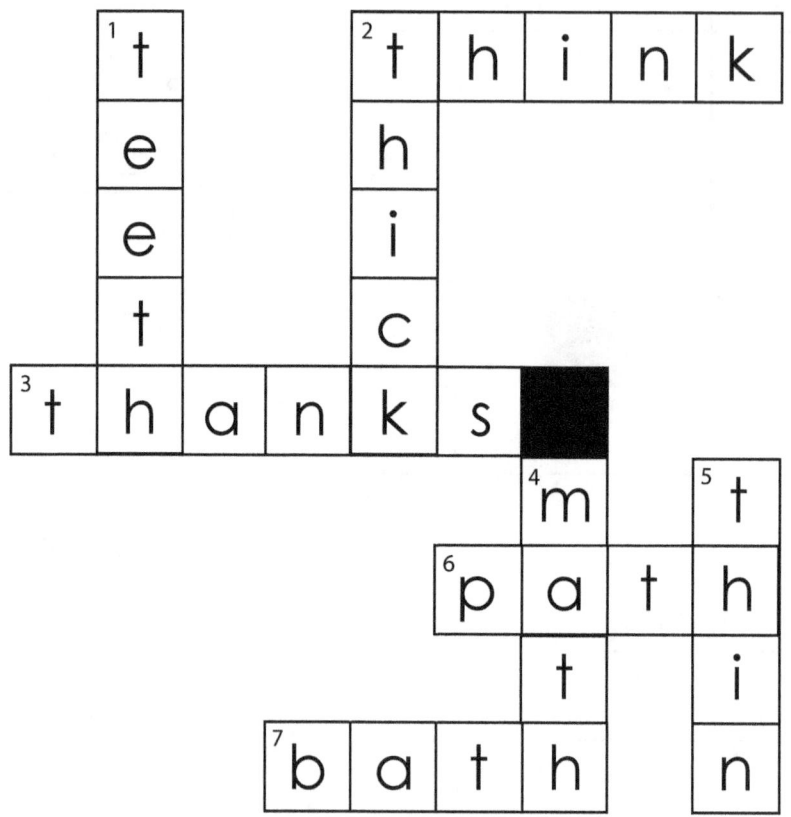

Circle the letters

Say: "**Circle the correct letters. Then write the word.**" T
Tell the child the pictures show: bath, path, math, teeth, think, thick.

(b) m r (a) x (t) m (h)   b a t h

i p a n x t m h   _ _ _ _

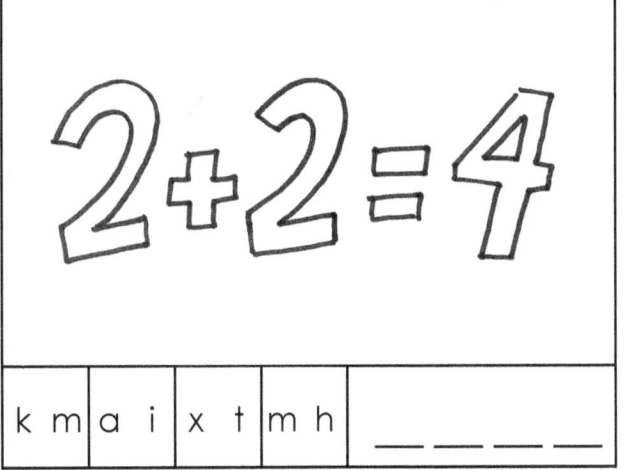

k m a i x t m h   _ _ _ _

b t i e n e (th)   _ _ _ _ _

(th) i h i n c k   _ _ _ _ _

(th) i h i c n k   _ _ _ _ _

75

Play the -th board game!

First one to reach the end wins!

| Instructions |

Materials you will need: • A single die.
 • Coins to use as markers.
 • Gameboard, *opposite page*.

1. Each player places a coin on "start."
2. Take turns rolling the die.
3. Move forward the same amount of spaces as the number on the die.
4. As you move forward on the board, read the words that you pass and land on.
5. For example, if a five comes up on the die, move five spaces on the game board and read five words.
6. The first person to reach the end wins.

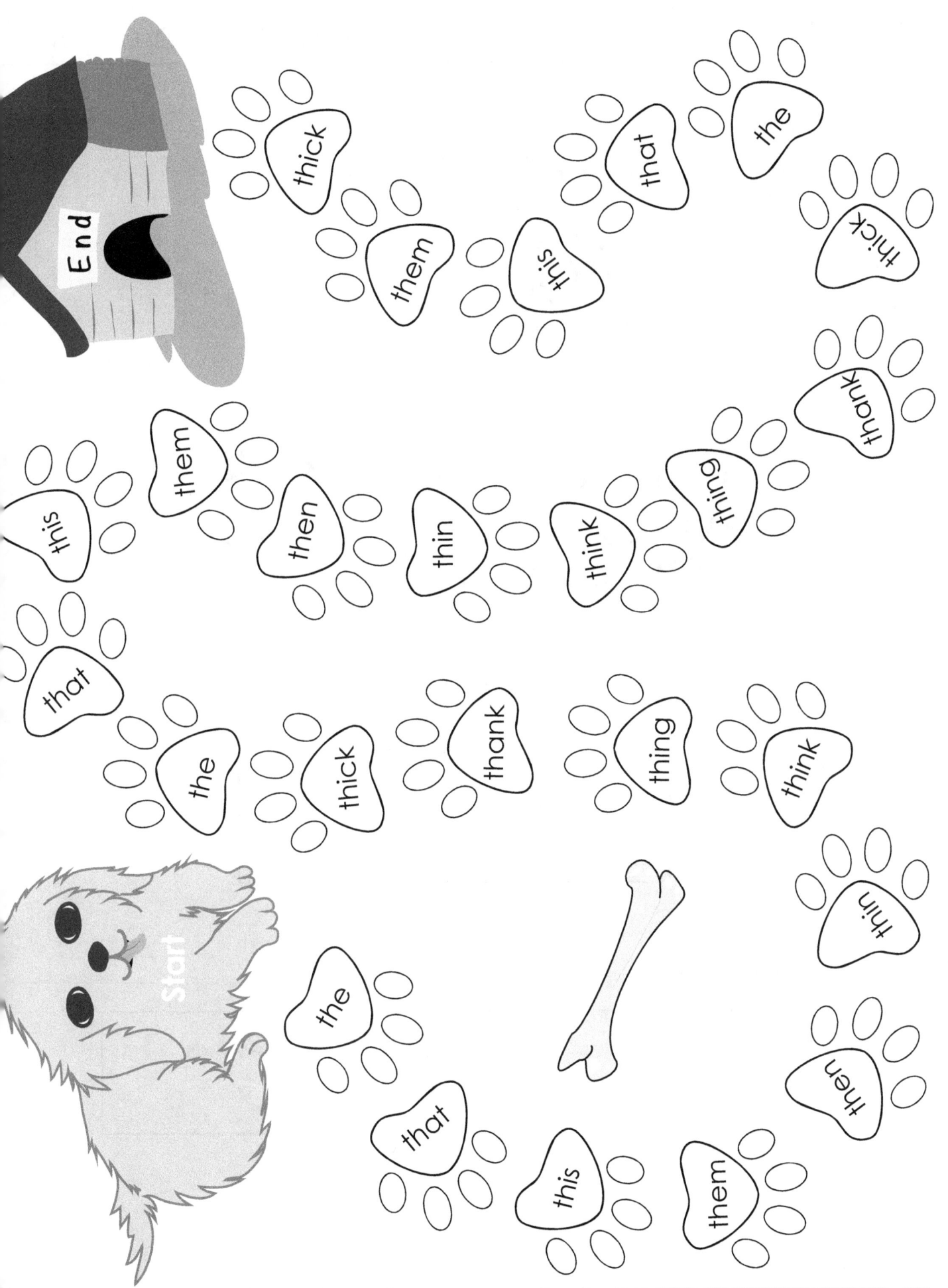

Step 7   The sound of 'wh'

'wh' says
'w' as in whale

Instructions

Say to the child: "**The letters 'wh' say 'w' as in the words what, wheel, and whale.**"

Beginning Sounds

Say: **"Write the letters that stand for the beginning sound of each picture. The pictures show: whale, chick, think, ship, thorn, whistle, chip, shed, and wheel."**

Play the wh- board game!

First one to reach the end wins!

Instructions

Materials you will need:
- A single die.
- Coins to use as markers.
- Gameboard, *opposite page*.

1. Each player places a coin on "start."
2. Take turns rolling the die.
3. Move forward the same amount of spaces as the number on the die.
4. As you move forward on the board, read the words that you pass and land on.
5. For example, if a five comes up on the die, move five spaces on the game board and read five words.
6. The first person to reach the end wins.

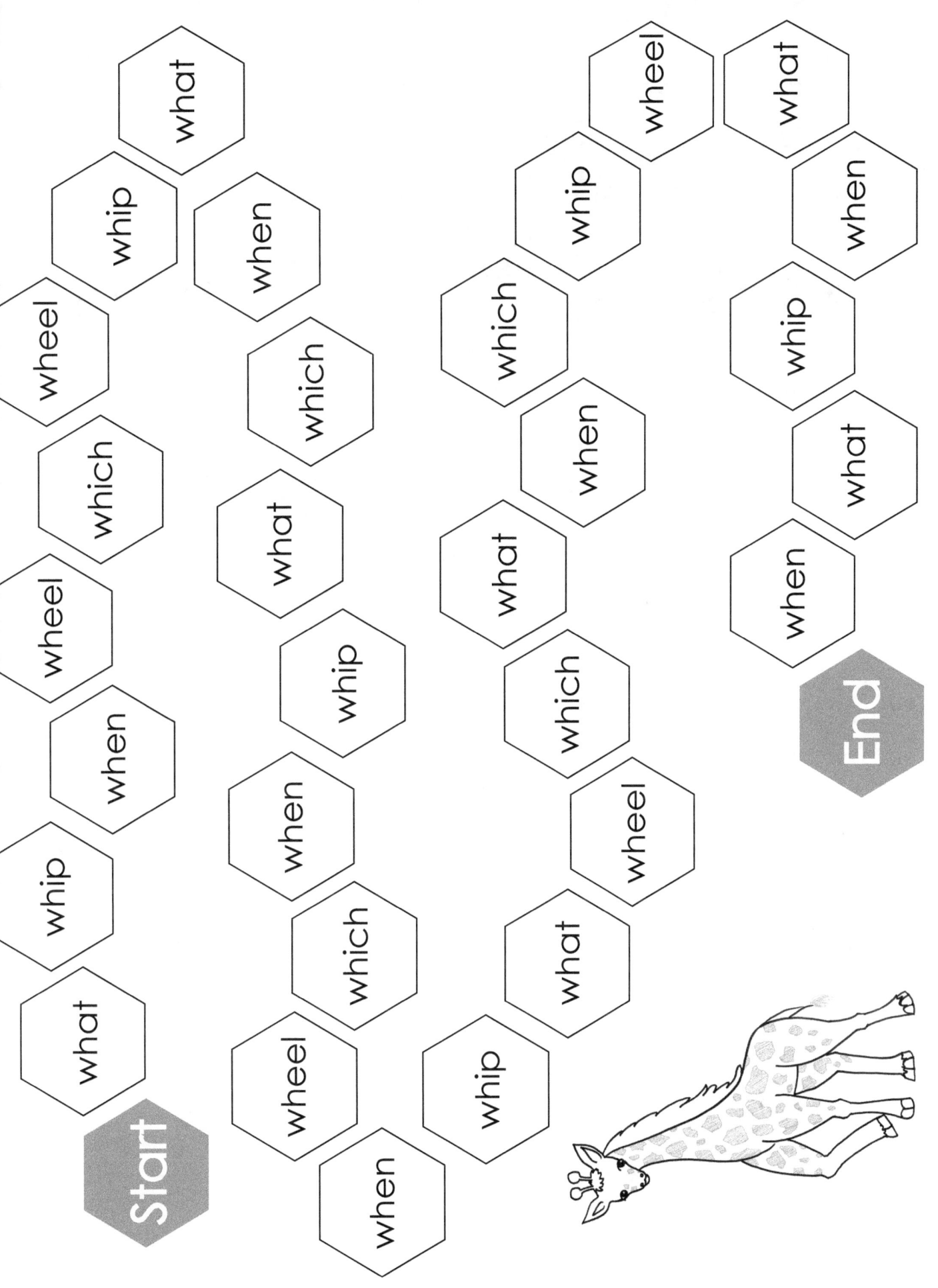

Step 8 — Power Word

what

what

what

what

What is that?

Instructions: Have the child read out loud the words below each picture.

What is that?
That is a chimp on a ship.

What is that?

What is that?
That is a dish on a bench.

What is that?

What is that?
That is a duck on the trash.

What is that?

What is that?
That is a fish on a dish.

What is that?

What is that?
That is a chimp on a bench.

Play Review Bingo

Instructions

<u>Materials</u>: • Flashcards. Cut out the cards on the opposite page.
• 2 gameboards follow the flashcards. In Bingo, every player gets his or her own gameboard. You and the child should each select a gameboard to use.
• Pennies to use as game pieces.

1. Place the flashcards in one stack, with the words facing up.
2. Have the child read the word on the top card in the stack.
3. Each of you should look for that word on your Bingo boards and place a penny on top of the word on your boards when you find it.
4. Place the card the child read face down on the table.
5. Repeat steps 2-4. The child should be the one doing all of the reading of the words on the flashcards. Continue until one of you has five pennies in a row, either horizontally, vertically, or diagonally. The first player to get five in a row should call out, "Bingo!" That player wins the game.

Play Bingo!

what	chin	the	shop	
ship	which	shell	when	dish
wheel	that	chest	wish	chill
bench	chip	pinch	think	chat
chimp	thick	chick	chop	this

This page is intentionally left blank.

This page is intentionally left blank.

BINGO

shop	chill	dish	bench	which
think	what	the	ship	wheel
shell	chat	✕	chest	wish
chick	when	chop	chin	thick
chip	this	pinch	that	chimp

BINGO

what	chin	the	shop	ship
which	shell	when	dish	wheel
that	chest	✗	wish	chill
bench	chip	pinch	think	chat
chimp	thick	chick	chop	this

Read a book!

Instructions

Read a book

The child can now read:

- "A Wish for Yak." This is book 15 in the Alphabet Series. See "Supplemental Materials," p. 1.

Congratulations!
You've completed Step 3 in reading!

Certificate of Accomplishment

Presented to _____

Date: _____ Signed: _____

www.ingramcontent.com/pod-product-compliance
Lightning Source LLC
Chambersburg PA
CBHW082244300426
44110CB00036B/2442